ROBERT RODRIGUEZ

A Real-Life Reader Biography

Barbara Marvis

Mitchell Lane Publishers, Inc.
P.O. Box 200 • Childs, Maryland 21916

First Printing

Real-Life Reader Biographies

Library of Congress Cataloging-in-Publication Data
Marvis, Barbara J.
    Robert Rodriguez / Barbara Marvis.
        p. cm. — (A real-life reader biography)
    Includes index.
    Summary: Presents a biography of the young Latino filmmaker who made "El Mariachi" for $7000 and went on to direct "Desperado" and "From Dusk Till Dawn."
        ISBN 1-883845-48-3 (library)
    1. Rodriguez, Robert (Robert Anthony), 1968– —Juvenile literature. 2. Motion picture producers and directors—United States—Biography—Juvenile literature. [1. Rodriguez, Robert (Robert Anthony), 1968– . 2. Motion picture producers and directors. 3. Mexican Americans—Biography.] I. Title. II. Series.
PN1998.3.R633M37 1997
791.43'0233'092—dc21
[B]   97-20752
                                                                                              CIP
                                                                                               AC

ABOUT THE AUTHOR: Barbara Marvis has been a writer for twenty years. She is the author of several books for young adults including the *Contemporary American Success Stories* series and *Tommy Nuñez: NBA Referee/Taking My Best Shot*. She holds a B.S. degree in English and communications from West Chester State University and an M.Ed. in remedial reading from the University of Delaware. She specializes in writing books for children that can be read on several reading levels. She lives with her husband, Bob, and their five children in northern Maryland.

PHOTO CREDITS: cover: Globe Photos; p. 4 sketch by Barbara Tidman; pp. 7, 8, 11, 12, 16, 22, 23 courtesy Rebecca and Cecilio Rodriguez.

ACKNOWLEDGMENTS: The following story is an authorized biography. It is based on the author's personal interviews with Robert Rodriguez and his wife, Elizabeth. It has been thoroughly researched and checked for accuracy. To the best of our knowledge, it represents a true story. Our sincerest appreciation goes to Robert and Elizabeth and Rebecca and Cecilio Rodriguez for supplying us with details and photographs of their lives.

Table of Contents

Chapter 1
Young Robert

Robert Rodriguez was born on June 20, 1968, in San Antonio, Texas. He has nine brothers and sisters. He is the son of Rebecca Villegas and Cecilio Rodriguez. Robert's grandparents moved to Texas from Mexico. Robert is the third generation of his family to live in the United States.

Robert liked growing up in such a big family. "There was always someone to do stuff with," he says. "If I ever got mad at one brother,

Robert's grandparents moved to Texas from Mexico.

Robert, at about five years old

there was always another one to play with."

Robert's mother liked to take all her children to the movie theater. Robert remembers seeing the same movies his mother said she had seen when she was growing up. Mrs. Rodriguez did not let her children see too many of the new movies out at the time. She liked the classic films such as the Marx Brothers comedies and musicals. "We'd sit with food hidden in bags of diapers," recalls Robert, "and watch the movies two or three times."

Robert did not pay attention in school. "I wasn't very good in math, science, history, in anything really," says Robert. Instead, he liked to draw cartoon characters

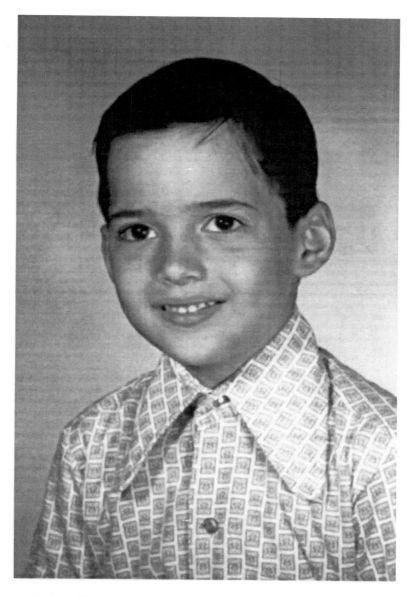

This picture of Robert was taken when he was about seven years old.

while his teacher was speaking. He had lots of fun creating little

Robert and his family are celebrating his birthday. Robert had lots of brothers and sisters to do things with when he was younger.

cartoon flip movies. "In fifth grade I remember sitting in the back of the room with a dictionary. I drew little stick figures in the margins. When you flipped the pages, my cartoon characters moved," says Robert. His friends would laugh at his paper movies. This made Robert feel good about himself, so he drew all the time.

Chapter 2
Early Films

When Robert was in eighth grade, he went to see the movie *Escape From New York* with some of his friends. After the film, they all decided they wanted to make their own real movies. The problem was they had no equipment. Robert tried to make a movie with his father's old super-8 film camera, but it did not turn out very good.

One day, Robert's father bought a new video cassette recorder that he thought he could use in his

Robert wanted to make his own real movies.

business. It came with a video camera. He gave the video camera to Robert.

Robert learned how to use the new camera. He made movies with clay figures. Then he made comedies starring his brothers and sisters. Everyone liked to star in Robert's films. For the next several years, Robert made all types of movies with his family and friends.

In high school, Robert became friends with Carlos Gallardo. Carlos was a boarding student from Mexico. Since Robert lived across the street from the school, Carlos spent many weekends at Robert's house. They would make short action comedies in Robert's backyard.

Robert says, "Believe it or not, I actually graduated from high school and got a scholarship to the

Robert and Carlos Gallardo made movies together in Robert's backyard.

University of Texas at Austin. My grades were never very good in school, but halfway through high school, I started earning As. I did well enough to get into college. My parents expected all their children to go to college. There was a film program at the University of Texas, so I went there."

While he was in college, Robert met Elizabeth Avellan. She was born in Caracas, Venezuela. She and Robert met in 1988 when Elizabeth was working in the vice president's office at the University of Texas.

Robert showed Elizabeth many of the movies he had made. Elizabeth loved the films. She thought he

Although Robert never thought he did well in school, he graduated from high school and went on to college.

should enter them in contests and film festivals. Robert was always too busy for such things. It was Elizabeth who would watch for word about the contests and remind Robert to enter them.

Robert and Elizabeth share many of the same interests. Elizabeth loves filmmaking, too.

One day, Robert entered his film *Austin Stories* in a festival based in Austin. He took first place. This was the beginning of his film career.

Elizabeth and Robert were married in 1990. Elizabeth eventually finished her college degree. But Robert found he was much too busy. His fame came before he could get the last two credits for his degree.

Chapter 3
Moneymaking Ideas

The first 16-millimeter film that Robert made was called *Bedhead*. It was about his brothers and sisters. It won several first-place awards in film contests. Robert would have liked to have shot 16-millimeter film more often, but it was too expensive. Robert was still in school. He had to earn money for school and for making this film. He learned that a drug research company paid college students to test their new products. Robert

Robert had to earn his own money to make his films.

volunteered for the tests. He used the money he earned to make his films and to buy books for college.

Then Robert had an idea to make a low-cost film. He wanted to practice making full-length films so that he could get a good job after college. Robert decided to film three mariachi movies. A mariachi is a Mexican street band. It is also a player in a mariachi band. Robert's idea was about a mariachi who played a guitar. Robert would sell the three movies to the Spanish home video market. Then he could earn enough money to make a big movie that would make him famous. But first, he had to find the money to make *El Mariachi*.

Chapter 4
El Mariachi

In the summer of 1991, Robert went through another drug study. The study lasted one month and he earned $3,000. He could not leave the test hospital for the whole month, so he decided to write his script for *El Mariachi* while he was there. He had lots of time to think about how he would make his new movie.

When Robert had finished his test study, he went to Mexico with his friend Carlos. Robert did not have

El Mariachi was Robert's first full-length film.

enough money to hire a crew or actors for the film. He and Carlos had to do everything themselves. Robert borrowed a camera. He found friends to act in his movie for free. Robert and Carlos decided Mexico was a good place to film because they would be running through the streets with cameras. In

Robert is filming El Mariachi. *He is giving directions to Carlos Gallardo.*

Texas, they might not be allowed to do this.

Robert had a lot of fun filming his movie. In one scene, Robert and Carlos borrowed a real jail. The police gave them permission to shoot real guns outside. While they were filming, one of the real prisoners was being loud. A guard took him outside so that he wouldn't disturb the film. The prisoner escaped! But they caught him later not far from town.

Robert could borrow the camera for only three weeks. He had to shoot quickly. Soon he was out of time. He had to give the camera back. He still had a lot of work ahead of him. Most cameras today record sound as well as picture. But the camera he had borrowed did not record sound. Robert had to record the sound separately on a

While they were filming at the jail, one of the real prisoners was taken outside. The prisoner escaped!

tape recorder and edit it together with the picture. This took him many weeks to do.

Finally, his film was finished. He showed it to Elizabeth. She liked it a lot.

Robert and Carlos set off to sell their film in California. They hoped to have it sold by Christmas. On December 1, 1991, they went to Los Angeles to look for a buyer. They had to drive nearly twenty-four hours to get there. They stayed with a friend, who let them sleep on his floor. They had no money for hotel rooms.

Robert and Carlos visited many film distributors. No one was interested in their film. But the friends did not give up. Every day, they went to see a new company to try to sell *El Mariachi*. Finally, a company called Mex-American made them an offer. It was the best they could get. They decided to take it. But when they went to sign the contract and pick up their check, they found the deal was not what they had thought. It was nearly Christmas, and Robert and Carlos could not be away any longer. They had to return home without having sold their movie.

It turned out that Robert was more successful than he had thought. While he was in Los Angeles, he had found an agent named Robert Newman. Newman liked Robert's film. He wanted to help Robert sell it. He began to show the film around to people he knew. Soon, Robert got a lot of attention. Many companies were interested in him. Walt Disney Pictures, Columbia Pictures, TriStar, and Miramax Films all wanted him

At first, no one wanted to buy Robert's movie. He kept trying.

to come to work for them. Robert's life moved into fast-forward after this.

Now when Robert had to go to Los Angeles, the big companies sent him on a plane and put him up in nice hotels. He didn't have to drive anymore, and he didn't have to sleep on the floor.

Columbia Pictures offered Robert a two-year movie deal, and they bought the rights to *El Mariachi*. Robert had his foot in Hollywood's door.

Robert was shocked at his sudden fame. "I never thought that *El Mariachi* would be my breakthrough film," he said. "I thought it was just a practice film so that one day I could make great movies."

Chapter 5
Fame

Robert received so much attention for *El Mariachi*, that it was 1994 before he made another movie. He filmed *Desperado* and *From Dusk Till Dawn*. Both movies were successful.

Despite his sudden fame, Robert has a very down-to-earth attitude. People like to work with him. They say he is a lot of fun. Robert likes to do much of the work himself. He writes the scripts, shoots the film, and then edits it. He sometimes does the work of five or six people.

Despite his fame, Robert has a very down-to-earth attitude.

Robert likes to film his movies himself. Here, he is using a Steadicam.

Nineteen ninety-five was a very good year for Robert. Elizabeth and Robert had a son, Rocket, who was born in September. They rented a big house in Los Angeles so that Robert

would have a place to
work on his movies.
Rocket and Elizabeth
went everywhere with
Robert.

Then Robert and
Elizabeth began
building a new house in
Texas so Robert could
work from home. In
1996, Robert and his
family moved back to
Texas to be near their families.

*Robert and
Elizabeth pose
with baby Rocket.*

"My parents were always very
supportive of anything I wanted to
do," remembers Robert. "They gave
me music lessons and art lessons.
But I never seemed to have any
talent in anything. It's funny how
things turn out. Making films
became my passion. My passion
has become my career."

Chronology

- Born June 20, 1968, in San Antonio, Texas; mother: Rebecca Villegas; father: Cecilio Rodriguez
- Began making films in junior high school
- Attended University of Texas at Austin
- Won the Third Coast Film and Video Festival for *Austin Stories*
- Made first 16mm film, *Bedhead*, which won many awards
- 1990, married Elizabeth Avellan
- 1991, made *El Mariachi* in Mexico for $7,000
- 1992, signed a movie deal with Columbia Pictures and sold rights to *El Mariachi*
- 1995, Columbia Pictures released *Desperado*
- September 1995, son Rocket was born
- 1996, directed *From Dusk Till Dawn*, backed by Miramax Films

Index